SCOTLAND'S PAST IN ACTION

Going to Bed

Naomi Tarrant

D1146951

NMS Publishing

Published by NMS Publishing Limited, Chambers Street, Edinburgh EHI IJF

© Trustees of the National Museums of Scotland 1998

Series Editor Iseabail Macleod

British Library Cataloguing in Publication Data

A catalogue record of this book is available from the British Library

ISBN 0 948636 96 3

Series design by NMS Publishing Ltd, designed by Janet Watson

Printed in Great Britain at the University Press, Cambridge

Acknowledgements

Illustrations: Front cover: Dundee City Council, Arts and Heritage Department and Alberto Morrocco. 5, 32, 34: National Trust for Scotland. 7: Scottish National Portrait Gallery. 9, 14, 26, 27, 31, 36, 37, 42, 43, 44, 45, 49, 54, 56, 58, 64, 65, 66, 68, 74, 77: National Museums of Scotland. 11, 17: National Gallery of Scotland. 15: Springburn Museum Trust. 22, 52: Royal Commission on the Ancient and Historical Monuments of Scotland. 29: Crown Copyright: Reproduced by Permission of Historic Scotland. 38: Lawrence Fine Art Auctioneers. 39: Bristol Museums and Art Gallery. 41: By courtesy of the National Portrait Gallery, London. 60: By permission of the Trustees of the Dulwich Picture Gallery. 69: The Fine Art Society. 73: The Paxton Trust.

Illustrations captioned SLA are from the Scottish Life Archive in the National Museums of Scotland.

Front cover: *The Attic Bedroom* by Alberto Morrocco, 1955.

CONTENTS

GOING TO BED

1 Introduction

Beds served not only as places to sleep but, because they were often the most substantial item of furniture in a room, they were also used for important events in a person's life and even as receiving rooms. Plenty has been written on the bed as an item of furniture or on the furnishing of bedrooms, but very little on bedding or the daily ritual, the act of going to bed. We spend about a third of our lives in bed so that the rituals of bedtime are important for they give a finish to the day. Nevertheless it is hard to find evidence in Scotland for some habits. For example, there is a wealth of information in inventories on bedding but not much detail. We are rarely told how wide or how long the sheets are nor in which order the bed clothes are put on the bed. Other information is equally hard to come by: there is no information on exactly what time was considered bedtime for adults or children.

There is not the wealth of illustrative material for Scotland before 1800 as there is for other countries. Nor do bedrooms feature very much in those paintings which do exist for the early period. Bedrooms rarely get photographed when the rest of the house is done, so that even for the nineteenth and twentieth centuries there are few good illustrations. With these caveats the emphasis in this book is on the period from 1500 to 1900, with less detail given for the twentieth century where information is more easily found.

Carved wooden bedstead, in Gladstone's Land, Edinburgh, of the type made by Aberdeen carvers. At the foot is a carved kist. The room is furnished as it might have been in the early seventeenth century when such painted ceilings were fashionable. Below the frieze the stone walls were probably hidden by tapestries or hangings.

2 Importance of beds

The most important events in a human life are often referred to by anthropologists as rites of passage. Those rites of passage associated with the bed and the bedroom are the three great events in a person's life, birth, marriage and death. Today most people in Scotland are born in hospital and many also die there, whilst the ceremonies associated with marriage and the bedroom have been dropped, either because they have been judged indelicate or because they are inappropriate where the majority of couples have been living together.

Birth

In medieval times the birth of babies to royalty and other wealthy families was marked by various ceremonies designed to present the child formally to the wider world and, in particular, to the spheres of its father's influence. There were also ceremonies associated with the mother and her cleansing after giving birth, a ceremony which in the Christian church is known as churching.

A woman usually spent a week or so in bed after the birth of a child and then, when she had her strength back, a series of visits from family and friends would be held in her bedroom. Here the baby could be viewed and commented on, particularly if it was a first child or an heir. But the real reason for the visit was to congratulate the mother on her safe delivery at a time when child-birth was attended by many dangers for the mother. In grand families these visits were stately affairs, but in humbler homes they would be truly joyful for both mother and visitors.

This type of visit was typical for most European countries from the Middle Ages to the late eighteenth century but we have little direct evidence for it in Scotland. One rare description comes from Elizabeth Mure's papers where she records the recollections of her uncle, Mr Barclay. Speaking of the period round about 1700 in Edinburgh he recalled that it was customary in wealthier families for the new mother to receive formal visits from friends.

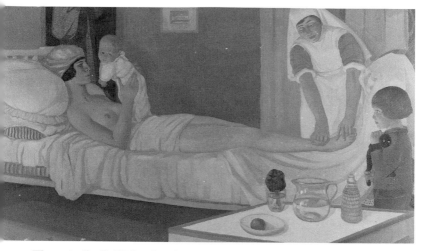

The artist Cecile Walton has depicted herself in bed after the birth of her baby in 1920. She is being given a bed bath by the nurse.

According to him on the fourth week after the baby's birth the mother was seated on her bed on a low footstool. The bed was covered with some 'neat piece of sewed work' or white satin and the mother was supported by three pillows at her back covered with the same material. She was in full dress, that is formally dressed, not in nightclothes, a cap on her head and a fan in her hand. Friends and family having been informed that the new mother was now ready to receive visitors on a particular day, they all came and paid their respects to her. As there were no chairs they had to stand or walk around the room. They were offered a glass of wine and a piece of cake and left after a short while so that others might come in.

This sounds as if the mother did not sit up in the bed but used it as a convenient way of being lifted above the throng with the bed drapes giving her a formal background, similar to a chair of estate. Formal dress in the early eighteenth century probably meant she was wearing a corset with a loose mantua draped, pleated and pinned to the corset, over a petticoat which showed at the centre front. Her head was dressed with a lace or fine muslin pleated cap with long lappets, that is pieces of the cap falling over her shoulders. A fan was always carried with formal dress.

Mr Barclay's account suggests that both men and women attended these visits to new mothers. Later on they seem to have become more informal and were mostly confined to women. George Penny in 1836 in Perth describes all the gossips crowding to a house when a baby was due. After the birth they made preparations for *the merry meat*. For this they made a pudding by putting into a large pot flour, butter, bread, ale and sugar. After this had been made the pot was filled with ale, brandy and sugar to make a hot drink.

Once babies were born in hospital more visiting went on there but the modern trend of short stays in hospital now means that home visiting has become more normal.

Courtship

Beds could also play a part in courtship. One such custom which is now obsolete is bundling. This was practised in several parts of Scotland as well as in England and Wales. It seems to have been particularly associated with rural areas where there were long cold winters and not much work to be done at that time of year. The aim of bundling was to allow young people to get to know each other but to prevent any sexual contact which might result in pregnancy. In areas with a scattered population it was not possible for couples to find privacy indoors in the warmth. There were no social clubs for them to meet in. So the young man often spent the night at the girl's home where the parents could make sure no impropriety took place whilst allowing the couple privacy for getting to know each other.

There were various ways of conducting this form of courting but in Lewis both the girl's legs were inserted into one large stocking and tied above the knees. The young man was then admitted into the bed where the couple could spend the night together without fear of a mishap. In the North-East the visit appears to have been more clandestine as the young man knocked at the window for admittance after the rest of the family had gone to bed.

Marriage

The custom most usually associated with beds and marriage is the bedding of the bride. This is a custom in many cultures with different variations, some of which are still practised in parts of the world, although it has now ceased in Scotland. Generally the custom here seems to have been that the bride was accompanied to her new home and put to bed by the guests. After she was undressed the bride would fling one of her stockings at the company and the one who caught it would be the next to marry. This took place after the wedding feast where the guests had no doubt consumed a good quantity of alcohol which meant it could be a very noisy and boisterous affair and this may explain why it fell into abeyance.

Edward Burt records a slightly different custom in the Highlands in the 1720s. For the first night after the wedding the young couple were relegated to a barn or outhouse, with straw, heath or fern for a bed and some blankets to cover them, while the rest of the company made merry in the house all night.

Green silk stocking, early eighteenth century, from Fingask Castle, Perthshire, said to be the kind worn by an unmarried elder sister at the wedding of her younger sister.

One of the most unusual instances of a bed being used in connection with a marriage is recorded by Susan Sibbald in her memoirs. She was living at Eildon Hall with her father in about 1801 and her uncle and aunt were living nearby at Benrig, near St Boswell's, when the event described happened.

It was apparently the custom when a female servant had been for any length of time with a family for her to return to her mistress's house the evening before her marriage even though she had been away at her own home for six months to spin her blankets and make ready what was expected as the 'the Bride's providing'. The marriage ceremony would then be performed at the house. Susan Sibbald, her father and sister were invited to Benrig when one of the maids was getting married. However a messenger had arrived from the minister [of St Boswell's] to say he was not well and therefore the ceremony must be performed in his bedroom.

Mr Sibbald and her uncle refused to go feeling that the minister should conduct the ceremony in his parlour, but the women at Benrig walked at the head of the bridal procession to the minister's house where they were escorted up to the bedroom.

> There was no other furniture in the room but a four post bed with dark green Moreen Curtains, which was in a corner of the room behind the door and against the wall. The curtains were closed all round except a piece open in front, the Minister perfectly invisible.
>
> When all had entered and the door shut, a voice issued forth as if from under a feather bed from its dull sound and asked 'Ar'ye all assembled?'

The bride and groom together with the best man and bridesmaid then went over to the bed, the couple joined hands and the minister asked them some questions to which no answers were required. The minister then gave an exhortation '...at the end of which a bow and a Curtsey from the happy couple towards the bed, and all took their departure...' from the house.

It was usual in most parts of Scotland for the bride to provide the bedding for her new home. In 1874 the Rev Walter Gregor recorded the *providan* of a North-East fisher bride. As well as a chest of drawers and a kist there was a feather bed, four pairs of white blankets, two pairs of barred blankets, two bolsters, four pillows and sheets.

Death

When there was a long illness preceding a death the bedroom became the focus of the household. Close relatives and friends might be summoned to come and take their last farewell of the dying person. Consolation in prayer and preparation for the future would be important aspects of the deathbed.

Detail from The Wake *by Alexander Carse, early nineteenth century, showing a body laid out on a bed, watchers by the bedside, and mourners coming to view the body.*

The Rev Donald Sage, for example, was taken as a small boy of three in 1792 to see his dying mother, although he had no recollection of this. Together with the other five children they stood round the bed to take leave of their mother and receive her blessing. Later, after she had died, he went into the room where her body lay on the bed covered in white and with white gloves on her hands.

After death in many areas of Scotland a lykewake was held, the sitting with the corpse until it was coffined. This was originally done to ward off evil spirits but was probably a practical necessity to make sure no animals attacked the corpse.

Elizabeth Grant of Rothiemurchus, in her memoirs of life in the Highlands in the early 1800s, described the body of an old man in his eighties, a distant relative, which she and her sister were taken to see:

> The body lay on the bed in the best room; it had on a shirt well ruffled, a night cap, and the hands were crossed over the breast. A white sheet was spread over all, white napkins were pinned on all the chair cushions, spread over the chest of drawers and the tables, and pinned over the few prints hung on the walls.

Beside the bed sat a watcher who offered visitors refreshments according to their rank. Meanwhile the widow received others in a spare bedroom. She sat there with her female friends whilst the funeral was being held as women did not attend funerals, as a rule, at this time.

Doctor's Visits

Home visits from the doctor could be occasions for much ritual around the bed, as Molly Weir recalled in visits paid by the doctor to her grandmother each winter when she was suffering from bronchitis. The night before the visit clean bed linen and nightclothes were laid out and the whole room cleaned from top to bottom. Next morning her mother got up an hour early and her grandmother was put into a clean nightdress, her hands and face sponged, the bed changed and the covers smoothed down. Molly was horrified when the doctor sat on the edge of the bed on her mother's precious bedcover which nobody was allowed to do. However, instead of being reprimanded by her grandmother for this lapse the doctor was welcomed and a prescription obtained for a good bottle which cured her of her bronchitis.

3 Scottish houses

The earliest houses, even for the wealthy, did not have many rooms. In most medieval homes rooms were multi-functional. In the poorest one room usually had to do for all domestic uses.

Most people in Scotland until the second half of this century have lived in one or two rooms. This is true of both the country-side and the town. In this situation both living and sleeping went on in the same spaces. However, where possible much of daily life was conducted outside the house so that the interior was very much a space for sleeping in and resting until quite recent times.

In the countryside there were single-room dwellings for the temporary summer migration to the hills with livestock, known as shielings. Single-space dwellings, benders, were also used by the travelling folk. These were tents which were easily transportable. Single male workers on farms lived in bothies which were sometimes just parts of out-buildings boarded off, but might be separate buildings. Usually these were fairly plainly furnished with beds and perhaps a chair or two with the farm labourers storing their possessions in their own kists which moved with them from job to job.

In the Highlands and Islands and elsewhere there were long single-story dwellings which housed animals at one end and humans at the other, although the humans usually had the larger area. Sometimes the single living space was divided by one or two box beds which gave a little more privacy. In the living area there might also be a settle which could double as a bed if necessary.

In Lowland cottages the box bed also served as a room divider. These were often placed with the foot ends together which would again give more privacy. With chairs and kists, for both clothes and dry goods, the rooms were fairly crowded. In the nineteenth century a distinctive type of chest of drawers developed known colloquially as the 'lum-chest' because it had a deeper drawer at the top for hats, particularly the tall men's hats which in the mid century resembled a factory chimney (lum).

Improvements in country dwellings for workers in the late nineteenth and early twentieth century gave people more rooms, one for living and one for sleeping, with slightly grander houses having a parlour, and perhaps additional spaces for coal and a pantry. However, all the living areas would probably have beds of some kind so that the maximum number of people could be accommodated.

In towns and cities houses were also small. Edinburgh had a particular problem because the space available for building was restricted to the rocky spine running from the castle to the Palace of Holyroodhouse. The buildings were therefore built upwards for several storeys, the various floors being occupied by different families. This pressure for housing often resulted in poorer families living in one room, several families to a floor, so that the houses became over-populated and unhygienic.

Late nineteenth- and early-twentieth century flats often had bed alcoves built into the kitchen or living room. Larger flats might have a box bedroom, with no outside window, slotted between front and back rooms. Storage space was gained by having beds fairly high so that boxes could be stowed underneath or a hurley bed, a low bed on wheels, could be slid under during the day. There was a mix of bedroom, dining room, sitting room and kitchen furniture all squeezed into a small space, yet there was still room for prized decorative items such as

Room-and-kitchen flat in Springburn, Glasgow, as it was in 1911. The kitchen has an alcove bed with curtains, patchwork quilt, white cover and a child reading. Other furniture includes swing cot, several types of chest, ornaments and dining table, showing the room's many uses.

pictures, photographs, vases and plants. Lack of possessions helped to make living in one room bearable, whereas the ability to afford a larger quantity of furniture would have made it much more difficult.

4 Bedrooms

In Europe houses were not formally divided into male and female areas in the way that they have been in other parts of the world, but certain divisions evolved to suit circumstances. There was a necessity to separate out safe areas in castles, for example, where the female members of the owner's family could pursue their tasks away from the boisterousness and danger of a largely military household. By the fifteenth century a private space for the laird and his family had been created in a small chamber off the main hall. This was known as a chamber of dais or chamber of dease and was a room which led directly off the dais, the platform where the top table stood in the hall. Many of the male retainers and servants would have bedded down for the night in the hall.

Privacy also gave the head of a household status. Visitors could judge their importance by where they were received. Reception in the private chamber indicated greater respect for the visitor or the person whom he represented. Monarchs in particular used this device, and the most important visitors were often received with the king sitting on his bed.

The most important piece of furniture in a private chamber was the bed, but the room also held a chest containing precious items, such as silver vessels or money, whilst other chests held clothes. The only chair might be one for the owner, otherwise small stools, the chests or seats in the deep window embrasures were used. Smaller beds for children might be slid under the main bed during the day.

There are no unaltered medieval castles in Scotland which show in detail how they were divided. It needs a trained eye to interpret the remains of these buildings. The later tower houses

Distraining for Rent, *by David Wilkie, 1815. The rather large,
bare room shows a disordered bed revealing the mattress and
blankets. Beside the bed is a washstand with jug and bowl.
In front of the table is a wickerwork cradle on rockers.*

dating from the sixteenth and early seventeenth centuries, of
which a considerable number still survive at least in part, show
the development of more comfort and privacy with several small
rooms used for different functions. The rooms which held beds
were still not used solely for sleeping in but more people had their
own room and their own bed.

Privacy became more important in the period after 1500, a
general European trend which was incorporated into Scottish
homes as its wealth increased, but was not something which was
considered necessary for all. Servants and children usually had to
share beds and both were heavily supervised by their employers
and parents for any lapses from moral and social order. There was
a lack of the kind of personal privacy which we value today.

However, the main motivation for those with power to create
private rooms was the desire for status, to set them apart from

those of lesser standing. In royal palaces and in the homes of the wealthy there developed a grand parade of rooms in the seventeenth century, designed to lead a visitor towards the most intimate room of the owner, his bedchamber, a term found in Scotland by the mid seventeenth century. It depended on the visitor's status or relationship to the owner how far they progressed through the parade. There would usually be a corresponding set of rooms for the owner's wife, the two sets often forming a balanced layout for the house, with rooms for less important members of the household fitted round them. Convenience was not the object of this type of dwelling: it was all show. In the eighteenth century, as attitudes changed and a genuine desire for more privacy developed, the houses of the wealthy reflected this. Grand parades remained but a set of genuinely private apartments might be added.

Changes over the last two hundred years mean that it is not easy to see any of the seventeenth-century parades surviving in their original form but an attempt at the Palace of Holyroodhouse, Edinburgh, shows how it was envisaged for Charles II in the 1680s. A more complete reconstruction can be seen at Hampton Court Palace, near London, in the apartments of William III. Seeing these royal apartments whether on a visit to Edinburgh or to London, or on an even grander scale at Versailles, was a stimulus to any Scottish nobles or lairds with pretensions to power. Some, like the Duke of Lauderdale who was responsible for overseeing the rebuilding of Holyroodhouse, even used the same craftsmen for his own new house, Thirlestane Castle, that were hired to work on the palace.

The eighteenth-century houses built in Scotland survive in greater number than those of earlier periods but they too have been altered over the years. Great houses like Hopetoun near Edinburgh, or Scone Palace and Blair Castle further north, show the way families have adapted their houses with changes in lifestyle. More complete documentation and plans survive from this period which help us to understand these changes better. But within a general picture each house is different, reflecting the changes in fortune of a family as well as practical issues such as the number of children or the ages of the occupants at different periods.

The convenience of one age is the inconvenience of the next, and the rate of rebuild or rearrangement in houses over a relatively short period of time can be quite startling. Newly married couples in the past were just as likely to want to make over an inherited ancestral pile as couples today are to want to decorate and furnish their new home to their own taste.

Use of the bedroom

As well as being a room for sleeping in, the bedroom was also used for entertainment and for storage, particularly of clothes.

Elizabeth Mure, in her recollections of life in Scotland in the eighteenth century, mentions how flat the young people found life in the country after the hectic social life of Edinburgh. They therefore

> introduced Colations after Supper; when the young met in some one of their bed chambers, and had either tea or a posset, where they satt and made merry till far in the morning. But this meeting was carefully consealed from the Parents, who were all ennimys to those Collations.

This fashion for collations stopped after about the 1760s.

5 Decorations

Although there is a general European trend in house styles for the wealthy, and in ideas of how houses should be arranged and in their furnishing, there are also great differences from country to country. Social divisions, wealth and cultural attitudes also determine how a house is divided and used. Only for the upper levels of society can we make any guesses for Scotland in the seventeenth century as we have very little evidence for the middle rank. For the majority of people, those at subsistence level and just above, we can extrapolate backwards from the more abundant evidence of the eighteenth and nineteenth centuries.

Fabric hangings on walls

From inventories we can get some idea of what furniture there was in various rooms in a house, but the actual decoration is not so easy to determine. Plain plastered walls can be cold and dull so to add warmth and colour to rooms wall hangings of various kinds were used. The very grandest were tapestries, loom-woven panels of varying size often in sets of seven or more pieces telling a story from the Bible or from antiquity. These were normally bought from the major workshops in France and the Low Countries, although there were attempts to set up tapestry workshops at Mortlake in London, with varying degrees of success. Tapestries could also be acquired secondhand as they were very hard wearing. There are many examples surviving in Scottish houses which have been in them for two or three hundred years, such as those at Prestonfield House, in Edinburgh, where a set of Flemish tapestries have been in an upstairs room since the house was rebuilt in the late seventeenth century.

Next in expense were probably embroidered hangings. These could be made in a professional embroidery workshop, for example the red wool pieces known as the Lochleven and Linlithgow hangings formerly thought to have been embroidered by Mary Queen of Scots. Or they could be made by a woman for her own home, as were the magnificent crewelwork pieces worked around 1719 and incorporating the cypher of James Stuart, the Old Pretender, and his wife Clementina Sobieska. Both the Lochleven and the 1719 hangings are virtually complete room sets, but other hangings survive as single pieces or as fragments in several Scottish homes.

Cheaper decorated hangings were painted cloths. These appear to have imitated tapestries, being painted with similar scenes. Plain cloth was used extensively in rooms, sometimes trimmed with braid or fringing, to match the bed. All of these wall coverings were made to be taken down and, if necessary, transported from home to home.

In the 1680s the Earl and Countess of Argyle had a house in Stirling near the castle. An inventory survives which details all the furniture and hangings they had room by room. The bed and its chamber had purple stamped hangings, which were probably of cloth printed in a self-coloured pattern. A recent restoration of some of the rooms, based on the inventory, gives some idea of how the lodgings might have looked.

Wallpaper

Paper for walls was not general until the eighteenth century, but there are examples known from the seventeenth century. There are twenty-three sheets of stamped paper for hangings mentioned in an Orkney inventory of 1710. They are amongst an incredible variety of items listed as found in the study of the laird, Sir Archibald Stewart of Burray, together with various pieces of bed furniture, clothes and maps.

Wallpaper was considered cleaner than fabric on the walls and was probably cheaper, but it was not until mechanization in the mid to late nineteenth century that wallpaper became possible for less wealthy families. Until then white- or ochrewash was more generally used for poorer homes. Bedrooms were always less lavishly decorated than the main reception rooms, except in very wealthy households, so that any wallpaper used in them was usually fairly plain.

Window Curtains

Window curtains were not general until the mid eighteenth century. Many windows had shutters so that curtains were not needed for either warmth or privacy. However, the 1506-7 royal accounts list forty-nine ells of sey (a woollen cloth) at two shillings and fourpence the ell for curtains for the baby prince's windows. Three iron rods and ten dozen rings were also supplied for hanging the curtains.

During the eighteenth century curtains became increasingly popular for all rooms. In the 1710 inventory for Burray, Orkney, there were four pieces of stamped (printed) calico at the windows in the Chamber of Dace (dais), with three stamped calico curtains at the windows in the White Chamber.

Pelmets, to hide the way the curtains were hung, could be quite elaborate and this trend continued into the nineteenth century. The principle bedrooms in large houses could have very elaborately draped decoration at the top and might also have blinds. Family bedrooms and servants rooms might only have curtains on poles with no pelmet. In towns, where bedrooms

Blue Room, Montgomerie House, Ayrshire, 1948, showing the accumulation of furniture a large country house bedroom acquired by 1900. As well as the bed, there are a variety of chairs, standing mirror, dressing table, towel rail, washstand and writing table.

might be overlooked by other houses, lace or muslin curtains, which were kept drawn, might be used to give privacy from the mid nineteenth century.

Curtains might match the fabric hangings of the bed, or later when bed curtains were no longer popular, they might match the wallpaper. However, in 1774 Thomas Chippendale supplied Ninian Home at Paxton, Berwickshire, with wallpaper to match the cotton bed hangings. Today there is a fashion for matching wallpaper, curtains and bedlinen.

Floors

Floor coverings in bedrooms were often of cheaper materials than those in the main living rooms. Scotch carpeting, also known as Kidderminster, was a type of double-weave cloth produced in several places in Scotland. It was hard wearing and because the design was reversible, it could be turned over when one side started to show signs of wear. It was produced in strips which could be sewn together to form a full-size room carpet, or left as runners along a passage or at the side of a bed.

Painted floorcloth is recorded in one bedroom at Melsetter, Orkney, in 1772. This material was the predecessor of linoleum, used extensively in the nineteenth and first half of the twentieth centuries for bedroom floors, much of it produced in Kirkcaldy, Fife. Linoleum and the modern version, vinyl, were favoured as they were easy to clean and did not harbour dust. For many poorer families it was cheaper than carpets, hard wearing and produced in colourful patterns. Today modern methods of production mean that carpets can be cheap to buy and they are warmer for bedroom floors.

Fires

Fireplaces were often put into purpose-built bedrooms but unless the owner was very wealthy fires were not usually lit in them. The Victorians considered fires in bedrooms to be unhealthy and were more likely to suggest that the window should be left open.

However, if people were ill fires were lit, but the grates were often small and therefore the warmth supplied might be meagre.

Bedroom decoration was finished by the addition of paintings, prints and, later, photographs to the walls, and with ornaments on the mantlepieces. Children's samplers and other embroideries were also framed and hung. In the seventeenth century the embroidered needlework casket, holding its maker's jewellery and small personal items, must have been prominent, although no inventory references for them in Scotland have yet been found.

6 Bedroom furniture

Storing Clothes

Clothes which were removed before going to bed had to be stored. For those who had very few clothes and little furniture this was not a problem. Many poor people, for example, would be wearing all the clothes they owned on a cold night.

Only the really wealthy would own enough clothes to have a choice of what to wear every day. For most people what they wore one day would be worn again the next, except on special occasions when they might have new or 'best' outfits to wear. However, if a person had more clothes these needed to be stored where they were kept clean, dry and away from any vermin. The simplest solution was a nail driven into the wall, found in bothies as well as in servants' bedrooms even in grand houses.

In the late nineteenth and early part of the twentieth century women might lay a piece of cloth over their underwear whilst it was stored overnight on a chair. This was supposed to be so that their husbands did not see their corsets, but Victorian homes were dusty from coal fires so the cloths would help to keep the white underwear clean. Airing clothes at night was seen to be important because it helped to stop them smelling fusty.

Clothes and other possessions were mostly kept in kists or chests, of various kinds and sizes, until well into this century. Servants would go from place to place with their kist which held all their possessions. Kists were also used as furniture in houses, often being covered with a cloth and turned into seating.

A kist was bought for the king's wardrobe in 1503 and at the same time twelve ells of small canvas was purchased to cover the king's 'clathes in the wardrob for cowm [dust] and dirt'. It is not clear if the clothes were put in the kist or hung up in some way in the wardrobe, which was a room and not a piece of furniture. The queen had twelve ells of linen for carrying cloths for her wardrobe, perhaps for wrapping round the clothes as they were taken to her.

The main disadvantage of a kist, as Elizabeth Grant points out, is the difficulty of getting at items at the bottom. Another problem was keeping clothes from getting too creased, although people in the past were not quite so paranoid about creased clothes as their twentieth-century descendants. However, for some fabrics, velvet for example, creasing was a real problem and delicate materials or trimmings could be crushed, thereby losing their freshness.

Another piece of furniture which could be used for clothes was the press. This had shelves in it which made looking for clothes easier than in a kist. Presses could also be built-in wall cupboards and it is not always clear which type is meant. In the inventory of General Tam Dalyell's House of the Binns near Edinburgh, taken at his death in 1685, there were two presses in the General's room, one containing estate papers and the other his clothes. The latter had a very varied assortment in it including boots and golf balls, but it mostly appears to be old pieces of clothing or night-gowns, informal wear, and not his ordinary wearing gear.

Presses could also be part of other pieces of furniture. One stand bed in the roup of Thomas Newal's goods in Dumfries in 1575 had a little press in the end of it, while an Orkney inventory of 1745 lists 'ane Sufficient bed with head and bottom, having a press in the end of it'.

Stand-alone wardrobes are found in eighteenth-century furni-ture makers' catalogues. At this period they usually have shelves at the top and drawers below. Some built-in cupboards in houses had large wooden pegs onto which clothes could be hung by the armhole. Coat hangers only came into use in the late nineteenth century, although dress skirts had had small hanging loops sewn in the waistband for many years. Mid to late nineteenth-century wardrobes often have small metal hooks inside onto which the skirt loops could be hung.

In the twentieth century wardrobes with shorter hanging spaces suitable for men's clothes developed. This was because men's jackets were not so long as women's clothes and trousers were usually hung over the rail of a coat hanger. Another innovation was to have separate drawers in the wardrobe for shirts, pyjamas, collars and gloves, with spaces for hats and shoes and a rail to hang ties over. There might even be small drawers to take collar studs and other small items.

As more people became wealthier they acquired more clothes and needed places to store them. Different types of clothing demanded new ways of storing. The high-crowned men's hats, which first appeared in the early nineteenth century, and the elaborate women's bonnets are two examples. Many more small items were needed, such as separate white collars and under-sleeves, and gloves were used in greater quantity than in previous periods. Chests of drawers and dressing tables were pieces of furniture developed to cope with the greater quantity of clothes.

Drawing of the inside of a wardrobe for women's clothes from The Workwoman's Guide, 1840. In the centre are sliding shelves for dresses with drawers below for heavy linen. The shelves on the right are for bonnets and shoes.

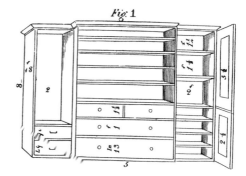

Fig. 1

Elaborate silver gilt dressing table set, French, second half of the seventeenth century. This set was owned by Frances Stewart, Duchess of Richmond, who lived at Lennoxlove, East Lothian.

Chests of drawers of various designs became popular during the eighteenth century. They had three or four long drawers with possibly two smaller drawers at the top. Chests became taller in the mid-nineteenth century with more drawers which could store clothes or household linen. Sometimes chests were combination pieces with a washing stand or writing slope hidden under the top.

Dressing tables with a central mirror were another eighteenth century fashion. Sometimes they were merely table tops with the legs hidden by fabric, with matching drapery surrounding the mirror. None of these survive but examples can be seen in portraits, for example in John Zoffany's portrait of Queen Charlotte and her two sons dating from 1764.

In the nineteenth century the dressing table developed into quite a specialized piece of furniture with several small drawers for jewellery, gloves, handkerchiefs and other little items. In the twentieth century triple mirrors became popular so that the back of the head could be seen by moving the mirrors. Dressing tables for women also had matching seats or stools, whilst those for men tended to be taller and have a single mirror.

Several inventories list writing desks at which ladies could write letters or check the household accounts. Washstands for holding basins and jugs, bedsteps for climbing into high beds, pot cupboards for chamber pots, mirrors of various kinds, comfortable chairs, small sofas, upright chairs and towel rails were all found in bedrooms by the late nineteenth century. More recently televisions, radios and computers have become part of bedroom furniture.

7 Beds

Beds were regarded by royalty and the nobility as more than places to sleep. Medieval miniature paintings often show royalty receiving petitioners or being presented with gifts in a room dominated by a costly bed. Sometimes the bed bears the coat of arms of the owner, either on the headboard or all over the hangings.

In 1503 King James IV married Margaret Tudor, the daughter of King Henry VII of England. In the Lord High Treasurer's accounts for that year are details of a great bed of state provided for the new queen at the time of the marriage. It must have been quite splendid and was certainly costly for it took seventy-seven and a quarter ells of cloth of gold at five pounds Scots the ell. It probably stood in the room described as the Queen's chamber which was hung with 148 and three-quarter ells of red and purple blue velvet at fifty shillings Scots the ell. By contrast the Queen's closet needed only forty-eight and three-quarter ells of scarlet and twenty-five ells of velvet for hangings and for the roof and head of another bed. This may well have been the bed the Queen mostly slept in particularly when the King was away on one of his many journeys. Another room had a partition of fifty-one ells of red, green and blue taffeta and a similar one was provided for the King. Partitions are mentioned quite often in the accounts and may have been used to give some privacy, possibly if there was not a separate garderobe nearby.

Although the accounts give us a vivid picture of the richness of the royal furnishings they give us no idea of how the various items looked, nor exactly in which rooms some pieces stood. Royal and noble households were peripatetic at this period and owners travelled from one residence to another, partly to eat up the rent paid in kind but also to oversee their estates. Much furniture was portable, because it was expensive to have several sets. All textiles could be transported from house to house and there are expenses listed in the Royal Accounts for carrying tapestries for example, between Edinburgh, Linlithgow and Stirling.

James IV was a restless man and travelled round Scotland almost continuously. Where there was no royal residence for him to stay in he would be accommodated at monasteries, abbeys or other nobles houses, though on occasion, and when on campaign, he had to use a camp bed. This is referred to as a *letacamp* (lit de

Reconstruction drawing by David Simon showing the Earl and Countess of Argyll's bedchamber as it might have looked in the 1680s, Argyll's Lodging, Stirling. The walls were covered in printed cloth to match the bed hangings.

camp) or *tursing* (carrying) bed in the accounts. The first mention is in 1494 but it was refurbished in April 1501 using variant taffeta for roof, curtains and pane (the piece hanging at the back of the bed). It was lined with fustian and heavily trimmed on the roof with worsted ribbons and silk and gold fringing.

Another notable bed supplied for James IV was one on board a ship, probably the *Margaret*. The King was very proud of his navy and was building it up. In the 1506 accounts the details given are for an English scarlet (wool cloth) pane, lined with grey fur, satin of Bruges stiffened with buckram and trimmed with fringes for the roof, green taffeta curtains lined in *trailze* (a checked cloth) and hung up with small green ribbons. Sheets, headsheets and fustian blankets were also supplied.

Aristocratic beds followed royal fashion and in the later seventeenth century the Scots were buying very grand state beds for their homes. Several of these survive including a particularly ornate one from Melville House, Fife, dating from about 1700, now in the Victoria and Albert Museum, London. In this bed the heavy red velvet curtains contrast with the lighter satin of the lining and bedspread, although the latter is encrusted with braid and applied decoration. The headboards of these beds often bore a coat of arms and the top edges were carved in fantastic shapes, covered in cloth and finished with bunches (panaches) of ostrich plumes at the corners. The weight of these canopies often required the assistance of supporting struts from the ceiling. Something of the effect can be seen in the King's bedroom at the Palace of Holyroodhouse in Edinburgh which recreates the appearance of the room in the newly rebuilt palace of the 1680s.

In early grand beds the plainness of the wooden frame is unimportant as it was covered by cloth. However, at the end of the sixteenth century there developed the heavy carved wooden beds, which today we think of as typical four-poster beds, though this term was never used until the nineteenth century. A particular style of this type of bed is associated with the Aberdeen school of carvers and an example can be seen at

Gladstone's Land in Edinburgh. At the top are richly carved side pieces where a cloth valance, or pand in Scots, hung to cover the loops of the curtains and their hanging rail. This rail is often missing from beds, taken off when they were modernized. The carving probably meant that the bed curtains were fairly plain but as there are no surviving examples we cannot be sure.

Another type of bed which was fashionable in Europe was the rectangular curtained bed known as a French bed. This has a simple wooden frame with curtains all round, a cloth roof with a valance round the top and one round the bottom, so that the entire

Blue printed linen curtain for a bed, eighteenth century.

frame is invisible. During the day it appears that the curtains were drawn back to show off the bedspread. Because they are merely a means of holding fabric and not themselves for display the basic bedsteads could be fairly coarse and have not survived, nor have their hangings. Although there are no illustrations of this type of bed in Scotland it is clear from inventories that it was common in the seventeenth and early eighteenth centuries, and was usually described as a cloth bed.

Standing beds, which appear listed in some inventories with hangings, are perhaps simpler wooden four-posters, but the term also seems to be used for the beds where the wooden frame was cut off just above the bed base and did not extend up to form a tester, or canopy. In the 1685 inventory of the House of the Binns, General Tam Dalyell's house, standing beds are found in the servants' rooms.

Tent bedsteads, mentioned in an Orkney inventory of 1747, are perhaps the small beds with sloping top which would fit under

Box beds for servants in the attic at Craigievar Castle. The shelves at the end were probably for their clothes.

the roof of a room in the eaves. With the curtains drawn round them they must have been very cosy in winter.

Box beds were known in Scotland at least from the sixteenth century. These beds were often built into a wall recess and were closed off with panelling during the day so that they looked like part of the wall. Later, in the eighteenth century, some box beds had curtains rather than panelling to divide them from the room; these could be used during the day as seating.

Small movable beds, which could be pushed under the main bed during the day, were often provided for servants. These were known as trundle, truckle, or in Scotland, hurley beds, and were also used in less wealthy homes for children and as extra beds for guests. Molly Weir, the actress, recalled in her memoirs sharing a hurley bed with her grandmother in the early years of this century in Glasgow:

> I couldn't remember a time when I hadn't slept in the hurley bed with Grannie. This was a bed on casters, which 'hurled' under the big recess bed out of sight during the day, and was hidden tidily out of sight behind the bed-pawn, ready to be pulled out at a touch whenever it was my bedtime. It was only about a foot off the floor, so that it could be hurled away fully made up with its sheets and pillows and blankets, and was probably made by a neighbour who

was a handyman joiner, and who grasped at once the necessity for using every inch of space in a room and kitchen which had to accommodate five people.

A small folding bed is mentioned in an Orkney inventory of 1710 but there is no indication of what it looked like. In some inventories press beds are mentioned and these were beds which folded up into the wall, probably into a press or cupboard, which could be opened out at night. In the nineteenth century the beds were often disguised as another piece of furniture, just as today the folding bed is likely to be a sofa or chair.

By the 1840s the types of bedsteads in general use according to *The Workwoman's Guide* included the four-poster, which had a wooden post at each corner; tent, a heavily draped four-poster; camp, a four-poster bed with a domed top; half-tester, bed with a roof covering only half the bed length; French pole, where the curtains are hung from a central pole along the length; French arrow, which had one long side against the wall and the curtains hung on an arrow; canopy, a bed with the drapery hung from a central boss; French block, where the canopy is hung from a square boss; turn-up, a bed folding up into a small space; stump, a bed with head board but no foot board and trestle, a bed on an X frame.

By the mid nineteenth century the four-poster and half tester bedstead were being replaced by one with wooden head- and footboard, often elaborately carved in mahogany, and with matching wardrobe, chest, dressing table, washstand and chair, forming a suite of furniture. Suites, containing varying number of items, remained very popular until the 1960s, when built-in unit furniture became commercially available.

In the second half of the nineteenth century iron bedsteads with coiled metal springs or a mesh base became popular. These were seen as less likely to harbour vermin and as they could be mass-produced they were used wherever large numbers of beds were needed, such as schools and hospitals. Fancy brass head- and footboards were also sold for more expensive beds.

Hill House, Helensburgh, designed by Charles Rennie Mackintosh, 1904, *showing the main bedroom with built-in head board and wardrobes.*

In the second half of the twentieth century the interior sprung mattress was introduced. This put springs into a deep padded cover with other springs in the base. These are usually sold as a base and mattress together, with head- or footboards chosen separately. Other materials which have been used are rubber and synthetic foam. These are particularly popular for those who suffer from allergies as the materials used in the more traditional mattresses often cause problems for hay fever and asthma sufferers.

Fitted bedroom furniture, where bed, wardrobes, dressing table and chests are all cut and fitted onto the walls, have been popular since the 1960s. They make it possible to fit the maximum amount of furniture into the smaller rooms of new houses.

Servants

Servants, until the eighteenth century, very often slept in the same room as their master or mistress, sometimes in an adjoining room, and at times outside across the doorway. This was partly for security but it was also useful to have the servant to hand if anything was required during the night. It was usually the most intimate body servants, valets or ladies maids, who slept so close to their employer.

Until the nineteenth century there were more male than female servants employed both inside and outside the house. In very large houses there was also a good number of indoor male servants up to the First World War. However, women tended to dominate the indoor staff after the early nineteenth century. Large houses usually had separate rooms for male and female servants where three or four might have to share beds as well as the room. Gradually separate beds were provided but the sharing of rooms continued for longer.

Outdoor servants never slept inside. It was usual for the unmarried stable staff to sleep in the stables, often in the hay loft. For example in the late 1740s John Macdonald,in his late teens, became a postilion at the livery stables of Mr Gibbs in Edinburgh

> '...Mr Gibbs...set his carpenter to make a bed-frame for me over the hay-stall, in one of the stables, and gave me blankets, bedding and sheets every month.'

In 1957 Lady Astor was invited to stay at the Palace of Holyrood house in Edinburgh as the Queen's guest and her lady's maid, Rose Harrison, went with her. In her memoirs Rose complained of the servants' rooms at Holyrood:

> 'My lady's room was everything I expected it would be, but my own left much to be desired. It was a tiny place at the top of the palace, with an iron bedstead, an old washstand and a nasty brown jug of cold water standing on it, a rush-bottom chair which I dared not trust myself on, and a threadbare mat on the linoleum floor.'

Rose was used to a much more comfortable style as the Astors were very wealthy. She was so indignant about her room and the general treatment she received that she considered writing to the Queen to tell her about the conditions. However, Lady Astor persuaded her against it.

Babies

Cradles were provided for babies. For James IV and Margaret's first child, the Treasurer's Accounts for 1506-7 make it clear that there were two cradles provided, one a great cradle of state with a cloth of gold cover, the other a little cradle which had a scarlet cover. Presumably the baby prince used the little cradle most of the time but was shown off by his proud parents to visitors in the great cradle of state.

An early seventeenth century carved wooden cradle with rockers has knobs at each corner for pushing it to and fro, and metal loops for the binding straps which were laced over the top to stop the baby falling out. It is typical of a type of cradle popular amongst wealthy households in the seventeenth century. Wooden cradles of different types went on being made until modern times.

Carved wooden cradle with rockers, early seventeenth century. The large knobs at the corners were to used to rock the cradle, the baby being held in by a binding strap threaded through the metal loops at on the sides.

Other cradles were made of wicker-work, plaited straw or rushes, much cheaper materials than wood. One good example of this form can be seen in David Wilkie's painting *Distraining for Rent*, 1815 (p17). *The Workwoman's Guide* of 1840 describes this type of cradle as a bassinette, and advises it should be covered with muslin.

In the nineteenth century cradles for the babies of the wealthy were often heavily draped with fabric, and might even have curtains. They were often on stands so that they could swing and the baby was at a higher level which meant that the mother or nurse did not have to bend down so far to pick up the baby. *The Workwoman's Guide*

Draped cradle from the Army & Navy Stores Catalogue, *1907.*

illustrates one which can be taken to pieces when not in use. The author also describes a travelling cot which she recommended for those travelling with young children. The size given would suit children not old enough for a proper adult bed.

Small beds do not appear to have been provided for children until the nineteenth century when cots were developed. Most children before this date had to share beds with their siblings. The twentieth century has seen the development of separate beds for each child and this has placed more emphasis on special beds for children such as bunk beds, one above another, and beds with sides to stop small children falling out in the night.

8 Bedding

Whatever the outward appearance, the real necessity of a bed is that it is comfortable to sleep on. Until the nineteenth century when metal bed frames became popular, the bed base was made

Miniature mahogany fourposter bed with lashed canvas bottom, late eighteenth century.

of four pieces of wood forming a hollow rectangle. The hollow was filled in by slatted boards, canvas pieces laced together or strong leather straps going from side to side. For example, the new bed provided for Queen Margaret in 1503 had forty-two ells of *Franch* (French) *girthes* provided by the saddler John Lethan. On top of this, to make them comfortable, various mattresses, or 'beds' as they are often described in inventories, were laid.

The bed James IV ordered in 1503 appears to have had two great down beds and two great *Levand* (Levant) feather beds with bolsters and best Brussels ticking and two mattresses which came from Flanders. The materials cost the equivalent of £43.10s Scots, and cost another thirty-five shillings to make and stuff them and transport them to Scotland. The King was not the only person to have bedding from Flanders; in the roup list of goods of John Moffat, minstrel, in Dumfries in 1570 a 'flanderis fatherbed' was sold to Robert Mckynnell for three pounds.

The bottom 'bed' was usually a straw-filled sack, probably with little shape. On top would be more tightly packed mattresses of wool or horsehair in strong linen or even leather covers which confined the contents. The stuffings were usually held in place between the covers by passing threads through to the other side and knotting them, often forming a decorative pattern of tufts on the outside of the mattress. Really grand mattresses might have

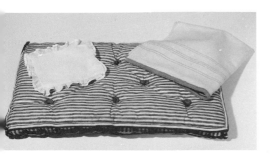

Miniature bedding made by a girl in Glasgow for her teaching diploma, 1910. The full set included mattress, mattress case, bolster, cover and case, two pillows and cases, two sheets, two blankets and a bed cover.

satin covers. Three or four mattresses could be used one on top of the other to form a comfortable bed. Over the mattresses might go a thin quilted satin cover, possibly to create a smooth base and stop the tufts from sticking into the sleeper. Surviving mattresses are rare but the early eighteenth-century beds at Hampton Court Palace near London all have a set of mattresses which it is thought are original to the beds.

In the mid nineteenth century it was recommended that the first mattress on a bedstead should be made of straw, very thick, and as hard as a board. These were always bought and were in a good strong ticking cover, at a cost of ten to thirty shillings. The second mattress, which could be made at home, was stuffed with horsehair or wool, although chaff, sea-weed, beech leaves or even paper were recommended for children.

Different levels of society had a greater or lesser number of mattresses. In 1796, for example, Trotter of Edinburgh supplied four mattresses for the bed of the Comte D'Artois, the French prince in exile who was staying at Holyroodhouse, three for the beds of his gentlemen, and two for the servants.

Bedlinen

Until the mid nineteenth century bed sheets would be of linen. In the largest and wealthiest households there would be several qualities of sheets. The finest were usually reserved for important guests. The next finest would be used by the master and mistress of the house, with their children having a lesser quality linen. The servants would have the cheapest linen but in very grand houses there might be at least two grades, with the upper servants getting sheets of a better quality than the lower servants. The very coarsest sheets, usually called harn, were given to the outdoor servants.

Again the royal accounts provide some information about habits in the early sixteenth century. In 1503 for the king's new bed seventy-two ells of Holland cloth at six shillings the ell was bought. This was the most expensive linen and was enough to make three pairs of sheets of three breadths each, each sheet containing twelve ells. Sheets of this width, that is three breadths of cloth sewn together to achieve the required width for the bed, indicate the size of the bed. Although the width of the cloth is not stated it was probably an ell wide, about thirty-seven inches or ninety-four centimetres, making 111 inches (212 centimetres) in total width. Other wide sheets of lesser quality linen were provided but it is not clear which bed they were for. Round (coarse) Holland cost four shillings and sixpence the ell whilst harn, the cheapest and roughest cloth, cost two shillings and ninepence the ell. The cost of making a pair of sheets was three shillings each.

Sheets were usually plain but top sheets might have some decorative edging of lace or embroidery. In the list of John Lorimer's goods rouped in Dumfries in 1575 there are two pairs of sheets with black ribbons, perhaps used for mourning or laying out the dead, and a sewed pillowcase, probably meaning it was embroidered.

These decorative sheets demanded more careful laundering, therefore it was more practical to make no distinction between the two sheets. In the nineteenth century it became the custom to put the top sheet on the bottom of the bed after one week so that only one sheet per bed was changed each week, thus making the most use of the linen before laundering.

Bolsters, long sausage-shaped pillows which went the full width of the bed, were popular in Britain until the 1960s. On top of them would be smaller pillows, or cods, as they are sometimes listed in the inventories. These were cases made of a strong fabric called ticking, which seems for a long time to have been usually black- and white-striped twill-weave linen, with cotton being used from the nineteenth century. These cases were then stuffed with feathers of various qualities. *The Workwoman's Guide* in 1840 lists chicken, goose and turkey feathers with goose down for the most expensive pillows. The very cheapest were flock and mill-puff, kinds of cotton waste used by the poorest. Households would keep the feathers from any birds they ate to use for stuffing pillows and mattresses. An Orkney inventory of 1747 lists seven bags of clean feathers, some containing down.

The actress Peg Woffington, painted in bed by an unknown artist, about 1758. A white satin quilted cover is shown on top of the bed.

*A set of matching five-colour striped cotton sheets and towels,
1960s. This very popular design was one of the first coloured
sheet sets on general sale.*

Linen or cotton pillow covers or beres were of similar quality
to the sheets. Until this century the covers were fastened by
lacing, ties or buttons. By the mid nineteenth century a strong
cotton undercover was recommended to help protect the pillow,
particularly feather pillows, as they are difficult items to clean.

Since the 1950s bedlinen and towels have become much more
colourful. Nylon and brushed nylon, in both pale and strong
colours, were popular at first because they did not need ironing
but they were too hot for summer use. The introduction of polyester cotton in the 1960s virtually ousted all other fabrics from the
bedlinen market as it washed well, did not need ironing and was
cool in summer. More recently cotton has made a comeback and
there are still people who prefer linen, even if it is difficult to
launder successfully in comparison to polycotton.

Blankets
On top of the sheets were laid blankets, which came in different
qualities and types. In the royal accounts quoted above there are
two different words used for blankets and for the fabric they were

*Fragments of heavy woollen fabrics which might be from blankets,
excavated from the lead mining site at Sillerholes, near Biggar,
date not yet confirmed but probably medieval.*

made from. *Quhit* (white) was bought to make *blanketis* and *fustian*
for *fustianis*, but both were white woollen materials, and it is not
clear what the difference was in their quality. Fragments of what
could well be blankets have been found at Sillerholes, the lead-
mining site near Biggar, which dates from the medieval period.

In Scotland in seventeenth- and eighteenth-century inventories blankets are often called plaids, sometimes bed plaids, and
are usually described as a pair. This means that they were sold as
a double length which could be cut into two or left as one and
used folded over. They were probably made of a white twill-
woven wool rather than being the tartan plaids we know today.
English blankets are also mentioned in some inventories and are
always more expensive suggesting they were of a better quality.
They may have been fulled and finished with a raised nap rather
like the later Witney blankets.

A particular type of blanket which appears to be Scottish is
an embroidered one. One example dating from 1705 appears to
be more a decorative cover for the top of the bed, but others are
less elaborate.

White wool blankets with various designs of blue stripes and checks at the ends, nineteenth century.

From the 1960s onwards duvets, continental quilts or downies as they are known in Scotland, started to replace sheets, blankets, eiderdowns and coverlets. Made of feathers, down or terylene wadding and with brightly coloured and patterned washable covers, usually of polyester and cotton, duvets reduced the weight as well as the number of bedclothes necessary for comfort.

Covers

A cover of some kind on top helped to keep the bedding clean. On a grand bed this often matched the bed hangings or the other soft furnishings in the room.

In the early eighteenth century bed sets of elaborately embroidered covers with a meandering yellow background pattern in false quilting were popular. As well as the bedcover there were often several pillow covers. Two or three pillows would be piled up and each cover would be more highly decorated than the one below. Fragments of these survive in many collections including one dated 1699 made for Margaret, wife of the Earl of Panmure.

Inventories list twilts (quilts), but it is not always clear how they were made. In Orkney Charles Stewart had a calico one in 1726 and Lady Steuart at Burray a Holland (linen) bed twilt in 1747, and two twilted blankets.

In the 1795 inventory of Alexander Henderson, a haberdasher in Leith, a patchwork bedcover and an old printed bedcover are

Patchwork quilt, of printed cotton hexagons, and a woven woollen bed cover in a small diamond design, both late nineteenth century.

listed. *The Workwoman's Guide* considered that patchwork, although durable, took up a good deal of time to make, but may be good work for schoolchildren. Patchwork quilts were popular in the latter part of the nineteenth and first part of the twentieth century. They has also been a revival of interest in this form of cover in the last thirty years.

Woven coverlets were also made in overshot weave where an extra coloured weft is woven over the background, usually creating geometric patterns. They were easy to make on a handloom and were still being woven in the 1960s. Scotch covers were probably similar to the double-weave carpets but made of a finer wool.

White bedcovers, or counterpanes, were popular in the nineteenth century. They were easy to launder and gave a fresh appearance to bedrooms. Some were made of machine-woven cotton with designs imitating quilting and are known as Marseilles quilts. Others were knitted or crocheted.

Eiderdowns became popular in the late nineteenth century until replaced by duvets from the 1960s onwards. Eiderdowns were usually fairly tightly stuffed covers which sat on the top of the bed adding greater warmth in the winter. Their covers were of various coloured fabrics, rayon satin being particularly popular in the twentieth century, and the best were made with genuine eider duck down. To keep the eiderdown anchored on the bed at night a sheet was often tucked over them.

In Shetland 'tattit' rugs were used as bed-covers from at least the eighteenth century but stopped being made in the 1930s. They consisted of a shaggy wool pile on a cloth backing and were made in two narrow strips which could be sewn together. This made them easier for washing. When too worn for the bed they were often put on the floor as rugs. Tattit rugs may be the later name for a caddow, sometimes an Irish caddow, terms often found in earlier inventories.

9 Times of going to bed

It is not easy to find out what time people went to bed in the past. Such details are rarely mentioned in letters, diaries and journals. There is a little more evidence for the time of getting up in the morning.

In the countryside the day would usually begin whenever daylight made it possible to start work. On farms the dairymaids went to bed about nine o'clock, as they had to get up early to do the morning milking. Anyone working with horses had to get up and feed and harness them first. This usually meant rising at about six but at the end of the day the horse had to be unharnessed, fed, watered and rubbed down. In summer this could mean a very long day, especially at harvest time when every minute of daylight would be used to get the harvest in.

Depending on how far they lived from school children had to get up early to get there in time. Many memoirs written about a country childhood in the early twentieth century speak of walks of three or four miles being not unusual, which would have meant that the youngest children would have to go to bed at about six o'clock in the evening. With schooling being compulsory for children from 1872 it was no excuse if there was a long walk to school at the beginning and end of each day.

Various trades and industries had their own times for starting and finishing work which dictated the length of the day for the workers. Throughout the late eighteenth and early nineteenth centuries the dinner hour for the upper classes became later and later in the evening, eventually settling at about eight o'clock. This meant that servants were kept up late but still had to get up early, especially the more general servant whose job it was to light fires and get the water hot for washing and early morning tea.

Shift work became a feature of factory work in the nineteenth century to keep processes going where it was impossible to close down a machine except once a year for an overhaul. Other factory jobs required long hours because the owners wanted to get the maximum amount of use from their expensive machinery. These long working hours meant that shops had to stay open late at night to accommodate their clients. It was not unusual in the nineteenth century for shops to close at ten at night on weekdays and midnight on Saturdays. This was still not the end of the day because goods on display had to be taken down and put away. The new day started at six am. The worst offenders were apparently the medium to cheap class of drapers and food shops who did most of their trade after the factories and offices closed. The fight to reduce the working hours of shop staff led in the twentieth century to the better regulation of their hours and the closing of shops for half a day a week as well as on Sundays.

However, everyone occasionally stayed up late for special entertainments. In the early sixteenth century James IV had three days of banqueting, after tournaments, which lasted from nine in the morning until nine at night. That was entertaining on the grand scale. In the late nineteenth century most public entertainment would finish before midnight, especially on a Saturday night, so that everyone could get home before Sunday. Theatres often took into account the last bus or tram times when they decided on the finishing time of their plays or concerts as there was no point in opening if the audience could not get home. For those who worked in occupations which were connected with evening entertainments the day would therefore finish late.

Travelling also meant that hours could be irregular. Late hours could occur from accidents on the road, trying to find a bed when none had been booked in advance or from the conviviality which meeting old friends might lead to. In 1803 Dorothy Wordsworth records that she and her brother, the poet William Wordsworth, arrived at Blair Atholl between ten and eleven o'clock at night after being refused accommodation at Faskally. They were touring round Scotland and had not booked in advance because of the uncertainty of roads and weather. Despite their late arrival '...we were civilly treated, and were glad, after eating a morsel of cold beef, to retire to rest...'

Another traveller in Scotland in 1803 was the poet James Hogg, who when staying with George Mackenzie of Dundonnel on Loch Broom records that 'We always remained at the punch-bowl until the blackbird sung at the window, as this was Dundonnel's rule, which custom he would not dispense with'. It is not clear for how long Hogg was there and therefore how many nights they stayed up.

Highland hospitality affected yet another traveller, James Boswell. In 1773 during his tour round Scotland with Dr Johnson, he sat up drinking punch until five in the morning at Coirechatachan on Skye and awoke next day at noon with a severe headache. However, the travellers had not arrived until eleven the previous night, just as their host and hostess were going to bed. Two nights later the rest of the house guests and the host again stayed up until five but this time Boswell was in bed and much disturbed by their drinking and singing 'Erse' songs.

10 Warming the bed

Linen and cotton sheets on a bed are cold. Fires were not usual in bedrooms unless the occupant was ill, old or very wealthy, so that going to bed in winter could be a chilly experience. Warming the bed before getting into it helped a person sleep more comfortably. It also helped to dry damp sheets, another hazard of unheated rooms.

Warmth in bed could be obtained by sharing. Many people had to share beds through necessity but as Molly Weir recalled when she had a bed to herself in a sanatorium:

> I had always been used to the comfort of a warm body to coorie [snuggle] into in bed, and it seemed chill and strange to find only draughty spaces in front and behind me when I tried to go to sleep.

The easiest and cheapest solution was to warm something in the fire which retained heat, such as a brick or stone, wrap it in a cloth and put it in the bed. Accidental burning was always a danger with this type of heating especially if the occupant of the bed was a restless sleeper. A similar device was the use made of a 'winter', the little steel shelf at the front of a range fire. This could be unhooked and wrapped in flannel so that toes could be warmed before getting into bed, as Molly Weir described doing in the 1920s.

Safer but more costly was the warming pan. These came into use in Europe in the fifteenth century. They were dishes of brass, silver or other metal with pierced covers and a long wooden

Warming pan of brass, German, eighteenth century, stoneware pig, about 1900, and two modern rubber hot water bottles, 1998.

handle. Live coals or charcoal were put in the dish and the pans were rubbed up and down the bed to warm it all over and to stop any part of the bed getting too hot. It was usually the job of a servant to warm the bed in this way just before the master or mistress got into it. Warming pans received some notoriety in 1688 when rumour spread that the long-awaited son born to King James and Queen Mary was not in fact theirs but another woman's child who had been smuggled into the Queen's bed in a warming pan. That child was James Francis Edward Stuart, the Old Pretender.

Stoneware hot-water bottles, often called pigs in Scotland, appeared in the eighteenth century and were popular until the mid twentieth century. They too needed a cloth cover otherwise the occupant of the bed could be severely burnt.

Susan Sibbald in her memoirs recounts an incident in the early nineteenth century at Dryburgh Abbey where the Earl and Countess of Buchan usually resided in the winter months.

> ... Lady Buchan had always a large canteen of hot water put into her bed, which was taken out before the Maid left the room after undressing her Ladyship.

One night, whilst a large number of guests were staying at the Abbey, the Earl stomped off to bed in a bad humour without taking a candle with him or calling for his valet. Suddenly there was a dreadful roar and the guests all rushed up stairs and

> ...there found the poor man in his sark sitting on the floor and writhing in pain, having come suddenly on the Canteen when he got into bed, and of course, being much scalded, but the violence of his anger against the Duchess [of Gordon] and other sympathizers was the cause of much merriment for some time.

The rubber hot-water bottle was introduced in the late nineteenth century but was not immediately popular because of the problem of leaks and the ease with which the rubber could be punctured. They did not last as long as the stoneware bottles and still needed a cover. Electric hot-water bottles were advertised in the Army and Navy Stores catalogues in the early years of this century but sound rather dangerous. The latest variation of the hot-water bottle is one which is heated in a microwave oven. It is not filled with water but with a chemical which means it can be used over and over again.

The most recent innovation for warming the bed has been the electric blanket which gives an even warmth to the bed. These gained great favour in the 1950s when they appeared on the wish list of wedding presents for many brides. Some types can be left on all night which is particularly beneficial for the elderly or those who feel the cold. However, the rubber hot-water bottle still continues in popularity. With central heating widespread in bedrooms though there are many who do not heat the bed at all.

Keeping cool in bed has probably rarely been a problem in Scotland. Usually fewer bedclothes and open windows suffice, provided proper precautions are taken with regard to any midges.

11 Washing the person

Personal cleanliness in past centuries is not easy to gauge. The writings of foreign visitors, or the tracts of those with a personal message to convey on a pet topic, may mislead about the general level of concern for hygiene. Both the countryside and the town were less sterile than their modern counterparts. However, people would be used to this and so a greater level of natural smells would be tolerated. Unusual smells might cause comment, for example, for those not used to the sea or the smell of fish, the stench of fish gutting or sea-bird droppings was difficult to stomach. So people got used to the smells of their own area and complained about those which were different.

It is clear though that some towns and rural dwellings had higher levels of odour than was generally acceptable and therefore there was a good deal of comment on these. Edinburgh in particular, before the New Town was built, acquired a reputation amongst both native and foreign visitors for its smell much of which resulted from the habit of throwing the contents of chamberpots out of the window. It was the emptying of these pots which caused so much concern to visitors when they walked through Edinburgh where the cry of 'Gardyloo' warned the walker below to beware as the contents of a chamber pot were about to be thrown out of a window. This was one of the disadvantages of living in a high rise building, as it was not easy to take rubbish down long flights of stairs.

Bedroom at Corehouse, Lanarkshire in the early 1950s showing the survival of a typical Scottish country-house bedroom of the late nineteenth and early twentieth centuries. To the side of the bed is a washstand with various jugs, bowls, basins and slop bucket, towel rail and mirror.

It is against this general background that personal hygiene must be seen. It is clear today that while some people thrive on dirt others find it very irritating and this was probably also the case in the past. Those who liked being clean managed to achieve it if they had enough money to afford the necessary equipment and time.

Washing facilities were usually housed in bedrooms until the development of the separate bathroom in the late nineteenth century. In the early twentieth century many wealthier homes had at least a wash-hand basin in the bedroom, but most others had to make do with water being brought into the bedroom in jugs.

Washing of the person was mostly confined to the hands and face. Baths were regarded by many as dangerous to health and were only taken at infrequent intervals, perhaps once a year.

In the medieval period, and later, baths were wooden tubs, rather like large barrels, and the water had to be carried to the tub in smaller vessels. In 1501 James IV's accounts show that three shillings was spent on 'ane pipe brocht to mak ane bath fat [vat]'. They do not tell us how often he used it.

Later royal accounts for Queen Caroline, wife of George II, who died in 1737, reveal more about the use and care of wooden bath tubs. They came in different sizes suitable for different tasks, such as foot baths, and if they were not maintained they would leak. It is also from these accounts that we get some idea of the other equipment needed for bathing. The tubs would stand on a floor cloth to protect the wooden floors and they were usually lined with cloth; linen or fustian seems the commonest. This prevented splinters getting into the skin. The bather might sit on a small stool inside the bath. After soaping the water was ladled up from the tub and poured over the bather. More curious though, seems to have been the practise of wearing some kind of clothing, possibly cut like a shift, whilst having a bath, a practise which still went on in some convent boarding schools until the Second World War. It was also considered essential for the bather to rest after taking a bath.

Queen Caroline appears rather eccentric in her enthusiasm for bathing but it is clear from accounts of palaces and other noble houses that bathrooms were not unusual in Europe. Henry VIII is thought to have had a Turkish bath at Hampton Court Palace, and in the seventeenth century there were bathrooms in all the main royal residences in England. The Duchess of Lauderdale installed one in the basement of Ham House in the 1670s, but there does not appear to have been one at Thirlestane, the Lauderdales' Scottish seat, nor at the royal residence of Holyroodhouse, which was rebuilt at this period. These fixed bathrooms had marble or metal baths and piped water, which were expensive to install and maintain.

Most houses which had a bath would have had a wooden tub, or later a portable metal one, which could be moved from room to room as required. The metal tubs came in different shapes and by the mid nineteenth century a great variety was advertised in trade catalogues. Hot and cold water for the tub was brought to the bath in receptacles known as cans. Baths were often placed in front of the fire so that the bather and the water kept warm and it was not too far to carry the hot water from the fire to the bath.

There was often a strict hierarchy for using the bath in poorer families. Where the husband had a dirty job such as coal mining

A selection of tin baths available through the Army and Navy Stores Catalogue, *1907.*

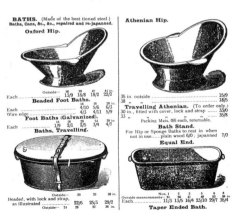

then baths were taken nightly, otherwise everyone bathed once a week. If there were several children then the girls would be bathed one night and the boys another. Next day clean underwear would be put on. In cities like Glasgow there was always the public bath house for those who lived in tenements. This was probably more practical for the adults in a family, although not necessarily very pleasant as the standard of cleanliness was not always high.

In wealthier homes the hot water was taken upstairs to the bather's bedroom where the tub would be filled by a relay of cans of hot and cold water. One guest at Rothiemurchus in the early nineteenth century bathed twice a day, which caused a good deal of annoyance to the maids. Later in the century constant hot water was provided by the boilers attached to the stoves in kitchens. Hot water was provided to the bedrooms in the evening for washing hands and face when the family changed for dinner, and again in the morning.

Showers were also used. In the mid nineteenth century portable ones could be placed in bedrooms and one is shown in a watercolour of Prince Albert's bedroom at Holyroodhouse. These portable showers had a round dish in which the bather stood, with a tank above filled by hand with jugs of water. There was a curtain all round and when the showerer was ready a plug was pulled and the water released over them.

From the 1920s onwards the greater use of makeup by women has meant that they had to clean this off their faces before going to bed. Various lotions have been used for cleaning and creams applied on the skin for the night. The cleaning of teeth is another twentieth century bedtime ritual.

12 Washing linen

Some people believed in being sewn into their underwear for the whole winter. But those who could afford it changed their linen regularly so that at least the clothes which came into contact with their bodies were changed frequently. It is not always easy to find out how often this happened or how frequently wash-days occurred. Many writers have quoted accounts which suggest this was done only once a year. However, whilst living in Inverness in the 1720s Edward Burt had his linen washed once a week.

Underwear had the double function of protecting the expensive, and often unwashable, outer clothing from the exhalations of the body, and protecting the body from anything injurious in the outer garments, such as dyes which ran or the scratchiness of certain fabrics. Underwear was therefore made of washable and bleachable white linen and later cotton, material which could be pounded to remove dirt without suffering unduly from the rough treatment which it received.

The washing of clothes and household linen was a labour-intensive and arduous job. The number of beds in a house and the quantity of table and other household linen, dictated the size of the job. Before chemical bleaching in the nineteenth century white linen was unlikely to have been the brilliant white which we associate today with white fabrics. Most linen was bleached

Drying linen on the green at Pittenweem, Fife, about 1900. SLA

outside by the sun usually in fields on the outskirts, where women could take the washing and lay it on the ground. In countries with indifferent sunshine for most of the year this might be difficult. The development of chemical bleaching by Tennants of Glasgow enabled bleaching every time the garment or piece was washed to be practical. The classic weekly-wash immortalized in the song 'Twas on a Monday morning when I beheld my darling...', became a late nineteenth- and twentieth-century ritual, only declining when the electric washing machine allowed working women to wash when it suited them.

In the tenements where a wash house was provided this had to be shared between eight, ten or more households depending on the number of flats on the stair. Molly Weir's family lived on a stair of twelve in Glasgow in the early years of this century, so their washday came round once every twelve days:

> With the meagre wardrobes we all possessed it must have been a nightmare trying to keep families clean and in dry clothes for twelve days between washing days... and a wet day a tragedy.

13 What to wear in bed

Sleeping in bed naked appears to have been common in the medieval period but the head was often covered by a cap of some sort. This may appear strange to us today but a good deal of body heat is lost from the head so that wearing a covering at night in damp or cold rooms makes sense. With modern heating and the better insulation of houses this is not so much a consideration, although in very cold weather some people do still wear a nightcap.

Nightcaps
It is not clear in the accounts of the royal household of James IV if nightclothes were provided for the king and queen, but the king is provided with at least one night kerchief for his head. These were probably lengths of linen which could be tied round the

head rather than made-up caps. Certainly medieval illustrations often show people wearing something more like a turban in bed than a cap. However, by the mid sixteenth century proper caps seem to have been worn, with ties under the chin.

Nightcaps worn in bed were made of plain linen or later cotton and after the wider introduction of the stocking frame, the machine-knitted cap or jelly bag was used. In darker colours these caps were also used by workmen and sailors, but white was usual for nightwear. It is not always obvious how the nightcaps for bed were made when they are listed in inventories. However, in 1803 members of the 1st Regiment of Royal Edinburgh Volunteers were ordered to have one worsted or flannel nightcap to tie under the chin, which suggests a close-fitting cap.

Dr Johnson tied a handkerchief round his head and this led his travelling companion James Boswell to remonstrate with

Two jelly bag night caps, the centre one of natural coloured wool the other of cotton. On the left is a Templar Cap, which buttons under the chin, mid nineteenth century.

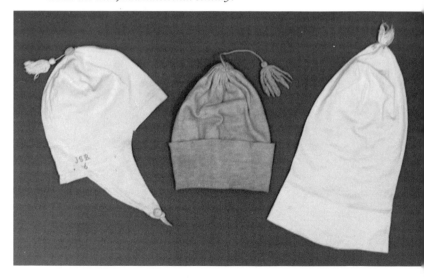

him when they were on their journey in the Highlands in 1773. Boswell asked him if he ever wore a nightcap and when Johnson replied no, Boswell pressed him by enquiring if it was best not to wear one:

> JOHNSON: Sir, I had this custom by chance, and perhaps no man shall ever know whether it is best to sleep with or without a night-cap.

Earlier Johnson had caught a cold and had been persuaded to wear a flannel nightcap which Miss MacLeod made for him. Boswell makes it clear that wearing a nightcap was the usual practice at that time so he was curious why Johnson would not wear one. It was seen as yet another example of the great man's eccentricity.

According to Martin Martin, writing in the early eighteenth century, men in Skye did not wear nightcaps before they were sixteen years old. Many never wore them all their lives and he believed this made them not so liable to headaches as people who kept their heads warm. Again this suggests that the wearing of something on the head at night was general.

Women also wore nightcaps but it is even harder to document these. They were probably plainer versions of their day caps and may therefore have changed with the fashions. In the seventeenth century, for example, it was not the fashion for women at Court to wear caps for most of the century although married women at other levels of society always wore a cap. However, in a painting by Van Dyck of Lady Venetia Digby painted on her deathbed in 1641, her nightcap appears to be plain linen with no strings to tie it under the chin, unlike the more usual day caps worn by women.

Nightcaps went out of fashion for both men and women in the second half of the nineteenth century although older people still wore them.

In the 1920s boudoir caps were popular. These were useful for keeping the short hairstyles neat as well as hiding any curlers. Before this date hair was curled using heated curling irons, but the small curlers, which could be slept in, were safer to use. Later, in the 1930s hair nets were used.

Lady Venetia Digby *by Anthony Van Dyke, 1641, in nightcap and night shift.*

Nightclothes

When nightclothes became general in Scotland is not clear. Probably the very poorest have always kept their clothes on at night in order to keep warm. Edward Burt, recording life in the Highlands in the 1720s, writes of a fellow traveller questioning a maidservant at their inn. She told him she never took her clothes off while they hung together. Burt was sceptical of this statement as he felt she would be forced to do so to deal with the vermin. She also said she had never slept in a bed.

However, Burt remarked on the fact that at one house, that of a prominent Highland laird, 'a young woman, as near as I guess, about seventeen or eighteen, who being surprised by the Light, and the Bustle we made, between Sleeping and Waking, threw off part of the Blankets, started up, stared at us earnestly, and being stark naked, scratched herself in several Parts 'till thoroughly wakened.'

Edward Burt was intrigued by the fondness Highlanders had for their plaid because it served many uses, one of them being to provide a covering at night. When travelling it was not always possible to reach an inn or a place with a spare bed so the plaid was spread on top of straw and the sleeper wrapped themself in it. This form of bed was called a shakedown.

Elizabeth Grant in the early 1800s records that the Spey floaters, the men who floated the logs of wood down river when it was in spate, from the Rothiemurchus estate, lived for the season in a large bothy with a central hearth and a hole above. At night each man lay down, on heather spread on the ground, in his wet clothes with his plaid wrapped round him and his feet to the fire. Their sleep was somewhat aided by whisky but it must have been an uncomfortable one.

As sleeping lowers body temperature anyway, clothes help to reinforce the warmth of any bedclothes. But sleeping naked appeared to continue in later times as some travellers' accounts make clear. One night in 1773, during his Highland journey, James Boswell debated whether to undress as he was not confident of the absence of bugs despite the fact that he had his own sheets. In the end he decided to plunge naked into bed as there would be less harbour for vermin when he was stripped. It seems as if he did not carry any nightclothes with him although curiously he did have a nightcap, so the medieval tradition obviously persisted.

James Hogg was another traveller who recorded stripping off all his clothes. He was staying the night in a cottage near Loch Broom and the cottager put down a heap of green heather for him to lie on and spread a pair of clean blankets over it. Hogg then stripped and wrapped himself in his shepherd's plaid before he covered himself with the blanket. Hogg was travelling on foot with very little in the way of extra clothes, only a spare shirt and two neckcloths which he stuffed in his pockets, so a nightshirt would have been an added problem.

When men and women wore night garments they were modifications of their basic underwear, the shirt and the shift, or sark as they were both known in Scotland. These are usually called night shirts or shifts, only much later did the term nightdress come to be used. They were made of similar quality linen to the day garments, but the nightshirts were usually cut much longer than the day shirt.

Women's day shifts followed fashion in the seventeenth and eighteenth centuries with low necks, but the night shift appears to have followed the male shirt in design with a higher neckline, collar and longer sleeves. The portrait of Lady Venetia Digby mentioned above shows one form of night shift. Lady Digby died in her sleep so she is shown dressed in what she wore for bed, unlike other deathbed scenes where the woman appears to be wearing more elaborate garments as if laid out for burial. Apart from a very fine pearl necklace and earrings she wears a plain linen night shift with possibly a collar, although the neck is open at the front, and long full sleeves, and a nightcap on her head.

Some woodcuts of popular ballads published in England in the mid seventeenth century show both sexes of the middle class wearing garments with long sleeves and high necks, as well as nightcaps. There is no reason to suppose that Scottish people of similar status did not wear the same kind of thing.

Usually a lesser number of garments was provided for night wear than for day wear. Two would be the minimum required so that one could be washed while the other was being worn. For example, a bridegroom in 1709 mentioned two fine Holland nightcaps in his shopping list. However, George Hume in 1694 records in his list of linens that he had six nightshirts, seven caps for nightcaps and three night cravats. It is not clear what exactly night cravats were, but probably they were wrapped round the throat to prevent chills.

In 1715 Lawrence Oliphant of Gask took three nightshirts with him on campaign but no caps. However, he had eighteen day shirts and an equal number of cravats. This shows prudence in providing a good quantity of linen when he might not have been able to get them laundered easily, but was perhaps rather excessive for taking on a military campaign. They could also have served quite well for bandages if he was wounded.

From the nineteenth century garments survive which tell us a little more about nightclothes. Both sexes still wore fairly plain shirt-like garments. Women's seem to have been made longer, to the ground, with a collar and front opening which was buttoned. The only decoration might be a frill down the front, round the collar and at the cuffs. *The Workwoman's Guide* shows another style of nightgown with a lower, wide neckline which the author considered more suitable for a sick person to wear when access to the neck was needed. The caps in this publication fit the head snugly with a frill round the face and they are tied under the chin.

Most nightclothes were made at home but by 1850 advertisements were appearing for ready-made garments, and the term nightdress starts to be used. Also by this time cotton, usually a fairly stout variety called longcloth, was replacing linen. From this period onwards many women's magazines give patterns for nightdresses and many of them had more decoration applied. Tucks, machine-made frilling and lace were the most popular. The style was still for high neck with collar, long sleeves with frills or cuff and an opening down the centre front to below the waist. Materials were still strong cotton and linens which could be boiled and bleached, but flannel was sometimes used for extra warmth. A mid-century innovation for men's nightshirts was a pocket on the left breast, possibly for a handkerchief.

In the 1880s Dr Jaeger's campaign to get people to wear wool next to the skin affected night wear and nightshirts and nightdresses in fine unbleached wool were advertised. The men's shirts were cut to the ankle with a buttoned opening to the waist, small collar and long sleeves with buttoned cuff. But Dr Jaeger also introduced a sleeping suit consisting of a pair of footed lower garments rather like modern tights, a top with a double panel over the chest, high neck and close-fitting hood for the head.

*Man's night shirt, about 1850. pyjamas, 1940s,
with Utility label.*

Pyjamas for men first appear in the late nineteenth century.
Originally these seem to have been cool silk or cotton garments
based on Indian patterns and used as informal wear in hot climates.
They were adapted for night wear particularly for travelling as
they were practical. Because they were shaped to the body they did
not leave any part uncovered. The Victorians considered it impru-
dent to sleep completely naked without any covering in very hot
weather as it was easy to catch a chill. Pyjamas were also useful
when camping as they cut down on unnecessary baggage but left
the wearer decently dressed if he needed to get up in the night.

By the beginning of the twentieth century men, particularly
younger men, preferred wearing pyjamas to nightshirts in bed.

Pyjamas were usually made of cotton or flannelette, but in the
1940s cotton mixtures with rayon or, later on, polyester were
introduced. Designs were either stripes or plain fabric, sometimes with contrasting coloured collars or piping. Wealthier men

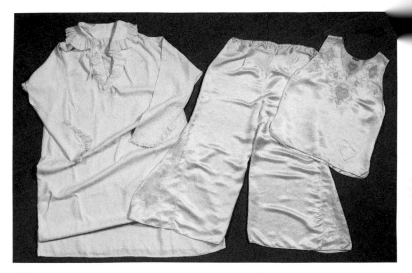

Women's nightdress, 1824 and cream satin embroidered pyjamas, made in Malaya, 1930s.

used silk pyjamas sometimes with their monogram embroidered on the pocket. Recently mens' night wear has become more varied with bolder designs and colours being introduced and new styles, including nightshirts and sleeping shorts.

Women's nightdresses in the early twentieth century became more decorative and made of a wider variety of materials. However, the majority wore fairly plain garments of cotton longcloth. Girls at school often had to make a nightdress as the culmination of their needlework courses. It was still seen as important that girls could sew at least the undergarments and night wear for their families. However, many of these nightdresses have ended up unworn in museum collections, which suggests that the styling was out of date or perhaps that the girls hated making them so much that they would not wear them.

Pyjamas for women were available in the 1890s but they were based on a one-piece combination garment and were not as

Black nylon nightdress and blue nylon negligee, Marks and Spencer, 1960s.

practical as a two-piece. It was not until the 1920s that pyjamas for women really caught on. Acceptance of them probably came first as lounging garments for indoor wear before they were used for sleeping in. Again their practicality for travel was probably a consideration in getting them accepted more widely; many women, such as nurses, had used them during the First World War.

From about 1920 onwards women's nightdresses became more decorative and also much more revealing. By the 1930s there was often no difference except in length between a nightdress and a petticoat. Sets of underwear often included a nightdress and they could be as heavily embroidered as any garment in the set. They were made of washable fabrics such as cotton, silk and rayon. After 1950 nylon was added to the fabrics and later machine-washable polyester cottons became popular.

Many girls in the period after 1920 wore pyjamas and when they grew up they tended to continue wearing them. However, most pyjama styles for women were not as pretty as the nightdresses. Baby Doll pyjamas were introduced in the late 1950s and became very popular with younger women and girls. These consisted of a very short, full waist-length top, usually with a low neck and no sleeves, and a pair of short, full bloomer-style bottoms, made in a pretty coloured nylon with lots of frills, lace and bows.

In the 1960s nightdresses started to make a strong comeback for women, helped by the new clothing styles whose influence and ideas spilled over into sleep-wear. One of these was the emphasis on Victorian fashions, introduced by Laura Ashley.

Today pyjamas are styled more like underwear, resembling a camisole top and French knickers, and some nightdresses look like large T-shirts. Nightclothes today are made in a variety of washable fabrics, colours and designs, very far removed from the white linen and cotton of the past.

In addition to body clothes, wearing a nightcap or bedsocks helped to keep these extremities warm. Most people find cold feet keep them awake so that wearing socks helped to warm up that part of the body. Bedsocks are not recorded in inventories but appear to have become popular in the nineteenth century. Patterns for knitting them are found in books and magazines and they are usually made a larger size than daytime socks and of thicker, fluffier wool so that air was trapped inside. Bedsocks are seen as a safer alternative to hot water bottles or electric-blankets and are therefore still worn by many people.

Dressing gowns

The term nightgown in inventories like the word nightcap can be misleading. Nightgowns were more like our modern dressing gown, worn for warmth when getting out of bed. They were made of heavier materials and were usually long. In time they came to be worn as informal day gowns by both men and women, sometimes to keep warm but often as a form of dress worn in the private rooms before dressing in the stiffer formal clothes worn in public.

Although there are no nightclothes for James IV mentioned in his accounts there are references to nightgowns, Queen Margaret had one of chamlot (fine wool) lined in fur in 1506. This would have been a good warm one which she could have used like a dressing gown. There is no indication of what style these nightgowns were.

Later nightgowns in the seventeenth and eighteenth centuries are cut very like Japanese kimonos. These garments started to come into Europe at this period through the Dutch trading links with Japan. Various fabrics were used including glazed woollen damasks (a speciality of Norwich), silk damasks and printed cottons. They could be lined and quilted for extra warmth.

Man's dressing gown of Paisley patterned fabric, available lined with flannel or quilted, Army and Navy Stores Catalogue, *1907.*

In the eighteenth century when men wore wigs, they shaved their heads for comfort. When in the home and dressed informally in a nightgown they wore decorative caps of embroidered silk or velvet, on their heads. These were called nightcaps. It became a convention to paint portraits of artists and writers in these nightgowns and caps, hinting that this was how they dressed when they worked.

In the nineteenth century the dressing gown developed out of the night-gown. They were more obviously bedroom wear, being used to go from the bedroom to the bathroom and worn over the nightclothes. They were made of woollen cloth for warmth or they could be quilted. Although they were often quite handsome garments they were not considered acceptable for informal wear.

Women also had bedjackets which they wore when sitting up in bed. These were a late nineteenth-century development and replaced shawls which were used in an earlier period. Wealthy women often had breakfast in bed and read their correspondence so needed something to put on their shoulders. A hand-knitted bedjacket was a popular present for a new mother in the twentieth century, particularly for those who went into hospital to have their babies.

Gwen in Bed *by James Gunn, about 1920. Gwen sits in bed in bed jacket and boudoir cap reading a book. On top of the bed is an eiderdown.*

14 Bedbugs

Bedbugs were a constant problem for householders. Jane Welsh Carlyle, wife of the historian Thomas Carlyle, becomes quite hysterical in her letters about the problems of keeping her house in London free from the pests. She dreaded leaving home in case the maid or her husband lowered their vigilance whilst she was away and the creatures made a return. Reading her letters today we might find them comic and pathetic in their vehemence but until well into this century bed bugs were a terrible plague to all levels of society, although a taboo subject in polite circles.

The bedbug (*Cimex lectularius*) is defined in the Oxford English Dictionary as 'a blood-sucking hemipterous insect found in bedsteads and other furniture, of a flattened form, and emitting an offensive smell when touched'. The bug appears to have become established in the British Isles by the sixteenth century and was widespread by the early eighteenth century when John Southall published his *A Treatise of Buggs* in 1730. Quite why they spread so widely is not known but contemporaries blamed the greater use of imported timber, particularly softwoods. However, there may have been confusion with other insects as identification was difficult.

The insects were found in furniture and bedding, as well as behind wallpaper, a new and increasingly popular form of wall decoration in the eighteenth century. When fasting the bug is flat and can therefore hide in very small cracks in all kinds of places, and lay eggs there. This made it difficult to dislodge and once it had infested a place it was difficult to eradicate. The bedbug feeds on human blood and when full is fat and round. The bite, like that of the mosquito, causes intense irritation and leads to very restless sleep.

There are numerous references to them by travellers in their accounts as they were an obvious hazard of travel both in Britain and abroad. James Hogg in 1803 during a tour of the Highlands spent the night at the inn at Invershiel where there was only one room for travellers to lodge.

> I got the best bed, but it was extremely hard, and the clothes had not the smell of roses. It was inhabited by a number of little insects common enough in such places, and no sooner had I made lodgement in their hereditary domains than I was attacked by a thousand strong.

However, Edward Burt once found to his surprise that he had 'no Inconvenience from those troublesome Companions' when he stopped at an inn in the Highlands in the 1720s.

It was recognized quite early on that the best way of dealing with bedbugs was to keep the house clean, particularly the beds and the rooms they were in. The rooms should be well aired to get rid of stale air, mattresses should be stuffed with clean materials, bed curtains should be regularly cleaned, the furniture rubbed down and hushed and the floors cleaned. Reading Jane Carlyle's battle with bedbugs makes sense of the very exhaustive instructions given in nineteenth-century manuals of housekeeping which to today's generation appear to be exercises in creating work to keep servants occupied. Neglect could mean an infestation of bugs which no one enjoyed.

The Workwoman's Guide comments:

> In providing bedsteads, it is always better to purchase them quite new, even when required for the commonest purpose, as those which are second-hand are liable to harbour bugs, which it takes both time and patience to get rid of.

Yet bedrooms became more and more crowded with furniture and knickknacks, all harbouring places for bugs. Although wallpaper was cleaner than textile wall coverings it was still not ideal unless regularly checked. Lighter washable fabrics for curtains of windows and beds replaced the old wool ones but velvet and silk were still used for the grander bedrooms. The press bed in the wall was particulary seen as a harbourer of bugs because it was difficult to air and difficult to clean out properly, the bugs being able to hide in the crevices between the planks. The emphasis on iron beds in the later nineteenth century and fresh air in the bedroom were both means of combating what was still a problem. Gradually bedbugs were eliminated from all but the poorest homes and became seen as a problem of poverty. The visit of the bug man was viewed with shame, but in the nineteenth century even Queen Charlotte had her Bug Destroyer.

15 Comfort in the night

Before the development of indoor toilets people had to use chamberpots and close stools at night or else make a long cold and dark journey to an outside privy. Chamberpots, made of various types of pottery and sometimes of metal, have a long history being found in many excavations of medieval sites in Scotland. Chamberpots in the nineteenth and early twentieth centuries were often part of a set for the washstand and could be quite decorative.

Chamberpots were used for liquid waste and would be kept under the bed at night so that they were near at hand. During the late eighteenth century special pot cupboards were developed the top of which could also serve as a bedside table. Below would be a small cupboard in which the pot would sit when not in use.

More substantial were close stools, or commodes, which usually had a metal pan and were housed in a proper chair. There was also a lid which when lifted revealed a padded toilet seat. Close stools were suitable for the elderly or the invalid, but they were also used for more solid waste rather than the chamber pot. If the close stool was being used regularly it might be housed in a small closet off the bed-room to isolate any smells, but it often formed another chair for the chamber and would be used as a regular seat. Some wealthier houses had close stools for the family so that they did not have to use the rather primitive outdoor facilities which would be all the servants had.

Earlier, stone castles and fortified houses had had chutes in the walls down which the waste matter would be discharged into a moat or onto the ground. These chutes, usually called garde-robes, can be seen in many ruined houses but the seats have gone so we do not know their exact structure. During his Highland tour Boswell stayed on Raasay where he saw the old castle. He felt in one respect it was superior to the new house; it had a garderobe whilst the house had no indoor sanitation.

The modern flushing toilet was not practical for most houses until a good water supply was available. From the 1850s onwards

Bedroom at Paxton House, Berwickshire, showing a restored mid eighteenth century bedroom with wardrobe and pot cupboards, the walls papered.

various means of producing a reliable flushing toilet which did not harbour germs was pursued. The Victorians, although embarrassed by too much talk about excretory matters, were strongly against germs and were therefore enthusiastic about improved sanitary arrangements. Whilst various possibilities were tried in towns and cities it was difficult in the countryside to install anything very complicated.

In rural areas earth closets were used but often the dunghill was considered quite adequate. Burt refers to seeing children come out of their huts in the morning, 'stark naked, and squat themselves down (if I might decently use the Comparison) like Dogs on a Dunghil, upon a certain Occasion after Confinement'. He himself had an unfortunate experience on one occasion

> for on rising early, and getting out of my Box pretty hastily, I unluckily set my Foot in the Chamber-Pot, a Hole in the Ground by the Bed-side, which was made to serve for that Use, in case of Occasion.

Even with an indoor toilet the use of the chamberpot continued for several reasons. One was the embarrassment felt at noisy flushing of the toilet which might wake up the rest of the house. Another

Wemyss ware chamber pot, twentieth century.

was the cold trip which might be necessary as the toilet was not always placed adjacent to the bedrooms, especially in an older house. In towns the tenements had one toilet to several houses; their condition could become very nasty and they were not very pleasant to visit at night. By 1900 country houses were building en suite bathrooms to the principal bedrooms making it quite comfortable and convenient to use the toilet during the night. Gradually, the use of the chamberpot declined as more houses acquired indoor toilets and better heating, so that today the decorative Victorian and Edwardian 'po' has become a collectors' item to be brazenly displayed for all to see.

For some people comfort during the night also meant having a drink to hand. This could be water or something more sustaining. Glass water carafes and matching drinking glasses were very popular from the late Victorian period onwards, and in wealthier homes each bedroom would be supplied with its own carafe and glass.

For those who liked warm drinks the French invented a very ingenious device, a *veilleuse*, which could keep soup hot all night with a candle burning under the dish. It sounds rather dangerous and there is no evidence that anyone used it in Scotland. However, the concept led to various attempts to design a means for providing a hot cup of tea to wake up to in the morning. Various devises were tried but the best was the 'Teasmade', an electric alarm clock and teamaker which, when the bell rang, boiled the water and tipped it onto the tea in a pot. The 'Teasmade' was regularly on the list of desired wedding presents for couples getting married in the second half of the twentieth century. The one drawback was remembering to fill it up with water the night before.

16 Reading in bed

For many people today reading for a few minutes or half an hour in bed before they settle down to sleep is a necessary way of relaxing. With safe electric lighting or even a small portable light which fits over a book it is a pleasurable activity helping to bring sleep closer by removing the stresses of the day. In the past, though, reading in bed was hazardous. Another dangerous activity was smoking in bed, something which became common practise in the twentieth century.

Bedrooms were often the last places to get electric lights so that until the early twentieth century most bedrooms would only have candle or oil lights. Candles were a great hazard in bedrooms unless protected by a glass globe, as the naked flame could be blown by draughts and catch bedclothes and especially curtains alight when these were used round the bed. Sometimes the reader would fall asleep without blowing out the candle which was very dangerous. Oil lamps were better as they had a glass globe but gas was never used as a bedside light so that even if the bedroom was lit by gas it was no use for bedtime reading. Even if bedrooms had electricity in the earlier part of this century it was often not the case that they had bedside electric lights.

Apart from reading in bed a light might be needed if for any reason a person wanted to get up in the night. A candle was the quickest to light once safety matches had been invented. Remember that it was not always easy to strike a light with flint and steel. Finding the way in the dark remained a useful skill.

Children are also often read to before they go to sleep. Again it is a good way to calm them down and make them relax. This kind of reading appears to be a nineteenth-century idea, part of the greater regard for children's education and seeing children as different to adults. The range of literature considered suitable for children grew during the century although most of it is too moralistic for present tastes. Many of the books that we regard today as children's books were seen as adult books suitable for children;

they had the equivalent of a PG rating, and would be read aloud to the whole family.

In the 1950s many children had portable radios in their bedrooms. One favourite pastime was listening to the Top Twenty pop music charts on Radio Luxembourg, huddled under the bed-clothes in case their parents heard them. Today children can watch television or videos in their own bedrooms, listen to music on CDs, or play computer games before they go to sleep.

17 Toys

Most children today have one or more toys they take to bed with them. They are a physical and mental comfort, often being make of a furry fabric which is soft and warm. Great anguish can be felt when a favourite toy is lost and sleep then becomes impossible for a time because the comforter has gone.

Quite when soft toys started to be made for children to take to bed is unknown, but like much else it was the Victorians who developed them. Few patterns are given for soft toys in women's magazines before the 1920s, but from then onwards soft toy patterns appear regularly. Pyjama, nightdress and hot-water-bottle cases were also made as soft toys. So essential were toys seen by mid century that many boarding schools allowed children to bring one with them to school as it helped to combat homesickness.

The favourite toy of most small children this century has been the teddy bear. This was developed in the early 1900s and there are various stories about its origin and name. Some believe it was named after President Teddy Roosevelt of the United States of America, who shot a bear but saved her cub. The German firm of Stieff produced most of the teddy bears before the First World War and many of those are now collectors' items. Adults are very attached to their teddy bears and many battered and worn examples can be seen on beds.

Today there is a more varied assortment of toys on children's beds. During the day toys grace the outside of the bed, sitting up,

Group of soft toys, 1950-1980. Private collections.

against the pillows. The numbers sitting on the bed during the day might well be many more than snuggle down inside the bed at night. All sorts of toys can find their way onto the bed in the daytime, from elaborately dressed dolls and plastic spaceships to oversized dogs. Even adults have their toys too, often very realistic animals of enormous size.

Live animals can also been taken to bed at night, although it is not considered healthy for children to do this. However, many adults share their beds with an amazing number of cats, or several dogs, or an assortment of animals. Like their inanimate counterparts they provide comfort and warmth and help to keep away the fears of the night for young and old.

18 Prayers

Saying one's prayers before getting into bed or at least before settling down to sleep was a general practise until fairly recently. Most families in Scotland would have prayers which everyone, including servants and visitors, had to attend, usually after supper. After these prayers anyone could go to bed who wanted to. Very small children might be excused these but they would be taught from a very early age to say prayers before they got into bed, sometimes kneeling beside the bed.

Bedtime prayers for children were something which the Victorians were particularly keen on although it is not an exclusively nineteenth-century practice. Usually children said their prayers aloud to whichever adult was supervising their bedtime and they were along the lines of asking God to bless the family. Older children might be asked to pray for a particular person who was ill or for a public figure, such as the monarch, or for the work of God in the missions abroad. If there was a war being fought in which the British army was involved then there might be prayers for the soldiers, with a special plea for any soldier known to the child who was engaged in the fighting.

Let us leave the last word to James Boswell, recording the end of a day spent with Dr Samuel Johnson on their tour of Scotland in 1773 when they spent the night of Tuesday 31 August at a house in Glenmorison called Anoch:

> After we had offered up our private devotions, and had chatted a little from our beds, Dr. Johnson said, 'God bless us both, for Jesus Christ's sake! Good night!' I pronounced '*Amen*'.

> He fell asleep immediately. I was not so fortunate for a long time. I fancied myself bit by innumerable vermin under the clothes; and that a spider was travelling from the *wainscot* towards my mouth. At last I fell into insensibility.

FURTHER READING

ADBURGHAM, A (intro) *Yesterday's Shopping: The Army & Navy Stores Catalogue 1907* reprint Newton Abbott 1969.

BEATON, E *Scotland's Traditional Houses from Cottage to Tower-House* Edinburgh 1997.

BENNETT, M *Scottish Customs from the Cradle to the Grave* Edinburgh 1992.

BOSWELL, J *The Journal of a Tour in the Hebrides* London 1785.

BURT, E *Letters from a Gentleman in the North of Scotland* 2nd edn London 1759.

CARRUTHERS, A (ed) *The Scottish Home* Edinburgh 1996.

CUNNINGTON, C W & P *The History of Underclothes* London 2nd ed revised 1981.

GRANT, E *Memoirs of a Highland Lady* new edn Edinburgh 1988.

SWAIN, M *Scottish Embroidery: Medieval to Modern* London 1986.

WALKLEY, C & V FOSTER *Crinolines and Crimping Irons: how Victorian clothes were cleaned and cared for* London 1978.

WEIR, M *Molly Weir's Trilogy of Scottish Childhood* 1988.

The Workwoman's Guide by A Lady 2nd ed 1840, reprinted 1975.

PLACES TO VISIT

Many of the houses in the care of the National Trust for Scotland and those privately owned houses open to the public show bedrooms. However, many have been altered over the years and do not show the rooms of earlier periods. The following houses show at least one bedroom in something like its original form, or have attempted to reconstruct one:

Near Berwick, *Paxton House*
Blair Atholl, *Blair Castle*
Culross, Fife, *The Palace*
Edinburgh, *The Palace of Holyroodhouse*, King's bedroom
Edinburgh, Royal Mile, *Gladstone's Land*,
Edinburgh, Charlotte Square, *The Georgian House*
Near Edinburgh, *Hopetoun House*
Glasgow, *The Tenement House*
Helensburgh, *Hill House*
Scone, near Perth, *Scone Palace*
Stirling, *Argyll's Lodging*

Many museums show furniture, clothing and other articles related to going to bed. Due to the nature of textiles it is wise to check what might be on display before visiting. The following are more permanent displays:

Edinburgh, Canongate Tolbooth, *The Peoples' Story*, has a common lodging house.
Kingussie, *Highland Folk Museum*, has items related to life in the Highlands.
Lewis, 42 Arnol, a furnished black house.
New Abbey, near Dumfries, *Shambellie House Museum of Costume*, displays various garments and linen in reconstructed bedroom and bathroom; also has a linen cupboard.